C is for Chinook

An Alberta Alphabet

Written by Dawn Welykochy and Illustrated by Lorna Bennett

Sleeping Bear Press
310 North Main Street, Suite 300
Chelsea, MI 48118
www.sleepingbearpress.com

Printed and bound in Canada.

10 9 8 7 6 5 4 3 2 1

Library of Congress Cataloging-in-Publication Data

Welykochy, Dawn.
C is for Chinook : an Alberta alphabet / written by Dawn Welykochy ; illustrated by Lorna Bennett.
p. cm.
ISBN 1-58536-223-9
1. Alberta—Juvenile literature. 2. English language—Alphabet—Juvenile literature. I. Bennett, Lorna, 1960- II. Title.
F1076.4.W45 2004
971.23—dc22 2004005500

This book is dedicated to Jim, Mikayla, and Katrina,
who are my greatest inspirations, as well as to my dear,
ever supportive friends Cathy and Kathy…
and a most wonderful editor, Jan.

DAWN

❁

For Austyn Joseph Locke
I'taamoisskitsipahpi
'One with a Happy Heart'

LORNA

A trader and an explorer,
Anthony Henday stands for **A**.
Who travelled across Alberta
the Cree would show him the way.

A a

Anthony Henday came to Canada in 1750 as a labourer with the Hudson's Bay Company. In 1754 he responded to a request from the governor of York Factory on Hudson Bay in present-day Manitoba. The governor had asked for volunteers to journey west to find out if the Blackfoot were willing to trap and deliver furs to the Hudson's Bay Company in exchange for goods such as cloth, metal tools, tobacco, and beads. The Cree Natives guided Anthony Henday on this difficult expedition up river and across the land.

Near what is now known as Red Deer, Henday met with the Blackfoot leader and made a fur-trading proposal. The leader did not accept Henday's plan because he didn't want his people to travel such a great distance from their home. As a result of Henday's expedition, the Hudson's Bay Company realized it needed to build posts in the west if it were to establish direct contact with Blackfoot traders. The Anthony Henday Museum is located in Delburne, Alberta.

B is for Alberta's mammal,
the mighty Bighorn sheep—
surefooted, agile, hopping cliffs,
climbing rock face so steep.

The magnificent and powerful curved horns on this animal give it its name the "bighorn." The male sheep are called rams and they have larger horns than the females, which are called ewes. The rams use their horns to battle other rams during the fall rutting (mating) season. Imagine rams weighing 114 kilograms ramming heads at 32 kilometres an hour! Fortunately they have two layers of bones around the brain, which are padded with a spongy mass.

The bighorn sheep's main predator is the cougar, but young sheep, called kids, have actually been carried away by golden eagles.

Some other common mammals in Alberta are the moose, which are the largest; white-tailed and mule deer; caribou; black and grizzly bears; mountain goats; coyotes; and elk.

Bb

Chinook winds come from the Pacific Ocean. They blow along the eastern slopes of the Rockies, funneling through the mountain valleys in southern and central Alberta. A beautiful cloud formation in the shape of an arch appears above the foothills, telling of the coming Chinook. In the midst of winter temperatures, a blanket of snow can disappear within hours as gusty warm winds blow. An extraordinary rise in temperature, up to 30 degrees Celsius, can actually occur within an hour, causing lakes or rivers to melt and break up in just a day. Chinook is a native word meaning "snow eater." Chinooks occur throughout the year but are most noticeable in the winter. Many of our winter days are affected by Chinook winds.

Cc

Warm Chinook winds are for C,
when temperatures 20 below
transform to a balmy 15 above
and they melt away the snow.

Dinosaur begins with the letter D.
Near the Red Deer Valley they roamed.
Today we excavate to find
raptor and duckbill bones.

Millions of years ago Alberta had a warm climate with lush vegetation. Plant-eating (herbivores) dinosaurs thrived here as well as (carnivores), those dinosaurs that ate meat, like *Tyrannosaurus rex*.

Paleontologists study prehistoric life forms and these scientists are still excavating in the Badlands of Alberta. Dinosaur Provincial Park is one of Alberta's, as well as the world's, best deposits of dinosaur fossils. Other major dinosaur bone discovery sites in Alberta include Grande Prarie, Grande Cache, Edmonton, Drumheller, Crowsnest Pass, Medicine Hat, and Milk River. Joseph Tyrrell discovered the first significant dinosaur fossil along the Red Deer River in 1884. The dinosaur fossils he found belonged to a fearsome predator, which was named *Albertosaurus* in 1905, the same year Alberta became a province.

Did you know that in 1987 in Devils Coulee, north of the Milk River, a young girl discovered some fossil fragments which turned out to be from duckbill dinosaur eggs?

Dd

Alberta's Famous Five—
these women made a plea
to be recognized as persons.
E is for Equality.

Ee

The 1920s was a time when women in Canada did not have many rights. They could not vote, nor hold a political office. They had very few rights to their homes or money, which they shared with their husbands. Five women in Alberta worked hard to achieve the recognition of "Women As Persons" under the British North American Act in 1929. They were Emily Murphy, Louise McKinney, Nellie McClung, Henrietta Muir Edwards, and Irene Parlby. Each of these women was a leader in her own right and organized women's groups, wrote books, helped write laws—all working to improve the status of women. Alberta's "Famous Five" helped achieve greater equality across all of Canada.

Ff

From a boat the fisherman casts,
as down the river he flows.
F is for Fly-Fishing
on a river called the Bow.

Glacial waters feed the Bow River from the Canadian Rocky Mountains. With the magnificent view of the Rockies, abundant wildlife, and a river filled with large trout, the Bow River is famous for fly-fishing. The Bow has a variety of trout that grow up to 70 centimetres long, one of which is Alberta's provincial fish, the bull trout. This trout got the name "bull" because its head is large in proportion to its body. A catch-and-release policy is in place for bull trout to protect it from becoming endangered.

F is also for our provincial flag. The shield, which is from Alberta's coat of arms, is centred on the flag. It displays the St. George's Cross and our many landscapes such as the Rocky Mountains, rolling foothills, and fields of golden wheat. The blue background represents our blue skies and is one of Alberta's colours along with the colour gold representing our wheat.

The great horned owl is one of the largest owls in North America, with a wingspan of 1.2 metres. Its prominent ear tufts and large size give this bird its name and its nickname, cat owl. It is commonly found in Alberta's forests.

Great horned owls mate for life and will lay one to five eggs. It rarely makes its own nest, and will steal the nest of a magpie or red-tailed hawk. Using razor sharp talons, this owl hunts at night as well as in the day, relying on its exceptional hearing and huge eyes to hunt rabbits, geese, and ducks. Great horned owls have a poor sense of smell and this is likely why it's a major predator of skunks!

On May 3, 1977, the great horned owl was voted Alberta's provincial bird of prey by children from all around the province.

Gg

G is for the Great horned owl,
who in the black of night
spots its prey with enormous eyes,
spreads its wings and then takes flight.

Sandstone pillars stand like rock giants.
Legend says from the valley they grew
and in the dark of night these giants awake.
The letter **H** is for sacred Hoodoos.

H h

Millions of years ago much of the interior of Alberta was under water. During this period many layers of sandstone formed. Later, flooding, flowing rivers, and strong winds carved through the soft sandstone, creating extraordinary rock shapes. These rock formations have been exposed for over 15,000 years and are ever-changing due to constant erosion.

Some legends refer to hoodoos as petrified giants that came alive at night to throw stones at unwelcome visitors. Some also believed the hoodoos were a sacred home to spirits. Hoodoos are scattered throughout Alberta, the major areas being the badlands: the Red Deer River, along the Milk River in the south, and near Tunnel Mountain in Banff.

And **H** is for Heritage Park, a large historical village in Calgary. Heritage Park's steam train operates on a more than 1,300 metre circular track. Halfway through each summer the train reverses its direction in order to even the wear on the wheels.

I is for the Ice fields
that reflect the sun's warm beams,
melting ice that flows to oceans
down through the mountain streams.

The Columbia Icefield is on the boundary of Banff and Jasper National Parks and is the largest body of ice in the Rocky Mountains. An ice field is a large body of ice that is formed from the compression of snow, forming glacial ice. Ice fields are usually found on the top of mountains due to the high altitude. The Columbia Icefield is what remains from a great ice shield called the Laurentide Sheet, which covered most of Canada 12,000 years ago. This ice field is surrounded by 13 of the highest mountains in the Rockies and feeds eight major glaciers. Ice fields and glaciers form when more snow falls than melts. An ice field may have meltwater streams flowing underneath or on the surface of the ice. The melting water then flows into the Pacific, the Atlantic, and the Arctic Oceans. The ice field is also a freshwater source for millions of Canadians.

I i

J is for cowboy John Ware.
He could wrestle a steer to the ground.
And a master at breaking horses,
the most courageous cowboy in town!

Jj

John Ware was a former slave in South Carolina who began his cowboy career in Texas. As part of a cattle drive in 1882 he came to Canada and the area that is now known as Alberta. John Ware was a big man and incredibly strong. In the spring of 1892 a longhorn steer started to charge several cowhands in a corral. They ran, all except John Ware who grabbed the steer's long horns. The steer then dragged him across the corral, but finally Ware brought the steer down. John was also superb at breaking wild horses.

In July of 2002 a special ceremony unveiled John Ware's cabin, which has been carefully restored. It is located in Dinosaur Provincial Park.

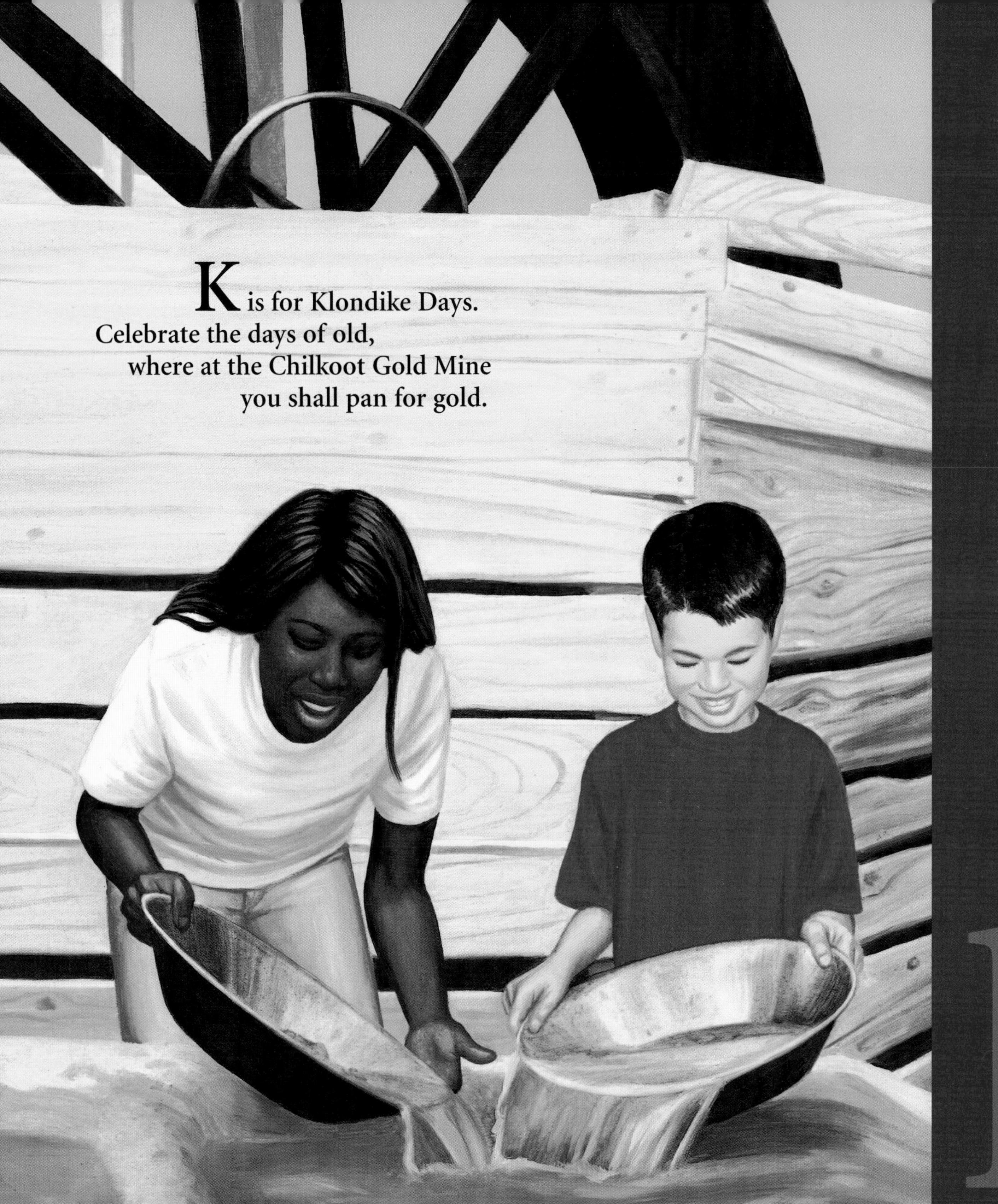

K is for Klondike Days.
Celebrate the days of old,
where at the Chilkoot Gold Mine
you shall pan for gold.

Klondike Days is an annual exposition in Edmonton celebrating the gold rush days. You can visit the Chilkoot Gold Mine—the Klondike era recreated—to learn the lost art of panning for gold. Over 700,000 people attend the fair every year. Events and programs include a Chuck Wagon Derby and nightly fireworks.

Edmonton is Alberta's oldest city, and was named the capital in 1905. In 1897 Edmonton became a frontier community and the "gateway to the North" for prospectors travelling north to the Yukon. Its name comes from Fort Edmonton, a fur-trading post. Today at Fort Edmonton Park visitors can see an exact replica of what stood on the banks of the North Saskatchewan River in 1846.

The Edmonton Eskimos (football team) have won 12 Grey Cups and Edmonton's hockey team, the Oilers, have won the Stanley Cup five times. Edmonton also has the largest mall in the world, West Edmonton Mall, with many extraordinary facilities such as its water and amusement parks.

kK

Lake Louise is sometimes called Canada's diamond in the wilderness and is located in Banff National Park. The Stoney Indians named Lake Louise *Ho-run-num-may*, meaning the "lake of little fishes." It was later named after Princess Louise Caroline Alberta, the fourth daughter of Queen Victoria. Mount Victoria overlooks Lake Louise and is 3,459 metres high and Chateau Lake Louise, built in 1892, is across the lake.

During the summer months many people visit the area to hike, mountain bike, and ride horseback on the trails that surround the lake. In the winter, the Lake Louise ski area is an excellent facility for downhill skiing.

L is also for the lodgepole pine, Alberta's provincial tree. Natives used this tree for teepee poles. Today this pine tree is still made into poles and used for many lumber needs.

Ll

A breathtaking view of Mount Victoria
from atop a tall pine tree,
an osprey spies a rainbow trout
and dives into **L** for Lake Louise.

Mm

When she was only 11 years old Mary Percy Jackson wanted to be a doctor and in 1927 she graduated with degrees in surgery and medicine. "Doc," as she was called, provided medical care for over 45 years in the Peace River country. She travelled by horseback, foot, and canoe, often in tremendous heat, to provide medical care. She also journeyed by dogsled, sometimes in bitter cold temperatures. Some common illnesses she treated were Rocky Mountain spotted fever, tick paralysis, and smallpox, as well as tending to broken limbs and tooth care. Many of her patients had immigrated from Norway, Ukraine, Russia, Germany, and Hungary. She cared for hundreds of First Nations and Métis and in 1975 the native women voted her "woman of the year." Doctor Jackson was often paid with moose meat, moccasins, berries, and beads rather than money. Dr. Mary Percy Jackson was a living legend, developed many lifelong friendships, and was dearly loved and respected.

M is for Mary Percy Jackson,
who travelled by way of horseback
over rough terrain to the injured and sick
with medicine stored in her saddle pack.

N is for First Nations,
there were many different bands.
Buffalo provided for their needs
while they lived upon the land.

Nn

The Blackfoot Confederacy was a union of First Nations in southern Alberta. These First Nations used buffalo (or bison) meat for food and its skin was used for clothing, bedding, and shelter. Tools, utensils, and decorations were made from the bones. Hooves were used as rattles and the bison's tongue was used in ceremonies.

Hunters would chase buffalo, directing them between lines of rock piles called cairns and running them over cliffs. One such cliff is named Head-Smashed-In Buffalo Jump, and is a UNESCO World Heritage Site. At the cliff base there are 10-metre deep deposits of bones. Nearby are hearths and boiling pits where the bison meat was prepared and cooked.

Today, Alberta's First Nations include: Dene (Dene Th'a, Chipewyan, Beaver, Tsuu T'ina), Cree (Plains and Woods), Nakoda/Stoney, Saulteaux (Ojibwa, Anishnabe), and Blackfoot (Piikani, Kainai, and Siksika).

An iron bit drops again and again,
pounding through rock and soil
to find what stands for the letter O.
Black gold, "bubblin' crude"...that's Oil!

In the late 1800s to the 1950s a cable tool rig was used to drill for oil. A heavy iron bit was dropped over and over again to pound through soil and rock. It could take two years to complete a hole 825 metres deep. Using today's tools, digging to that same depth would take just two to three days.

On February 13, 1947 "Leduc Number 1" blew into production, which at that time was the largest oil discovery in Canadian history. On a cold winter day with darkness approaching, the drill finally broke through after weeks of drilling! Black smoke poured out of the drilling stack and oil gushed out. It marked the beginning of the oil industry in Alberta and initiated the drilling of thousands of wells. Today the Athabasca Tar Sands near Fort McMurray are one of the world's largest oil reserves. The discovery of oil turned one of Canada's poorest provinces into one of the richest.

Writing on Stone Provincial Park near Milk River has the greatest concentration of rock art in North America. Painted rocks are called pictographs, and petroglyphs are rock carvings made with the use of antlers or bone. In later years metal tools were used. Red ochre was used for paint by crushing iron ore and mixing it with water and animal grease. Charcoal was also used to draw pictures. The petroglyphs and pictographs, both created on rock landforms, vary from 100 to 500 years old.

Shoshoni, Gros Ventre, and later Blackfoot believed powerful spirits inhabited this area. Buffalo hunters and warriors often returned to the site for spiritual guidance.

P is also for petrified wood, Alberta's provincial stone. This fossil formed when minerals in water infiltrated wood, replacing the organic matter (wood) with mineral deposits. The same structure is left behind and the stone looks like the original piece of wood!

Pp

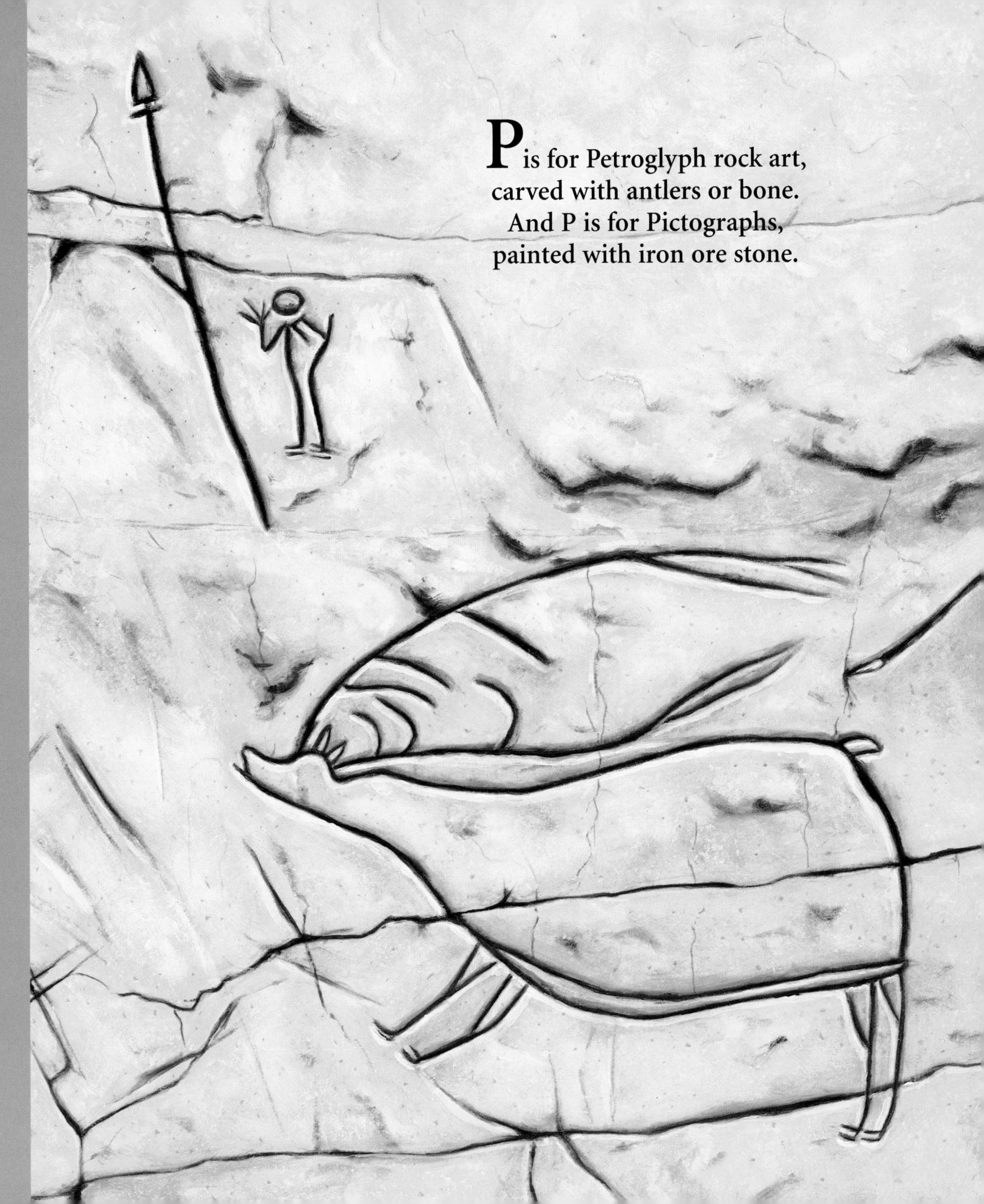

P is for Petroglyph rock art,
carved with antlers or bone.
And P is for Pictographs,
painted with iron ore stone.

During the glacial age about 14,000 years ago, geologists believe that a rockslide began at Mount Edith Cavell, near Jasper. Huge pieces of quartzite rock plunged down the mountain and landed on a glacier that was moving through the Athabasca River valley. Erratic quartzite are rock fragments that were transported by these glaciers and deposited in various locations as the glacial ice melted. A trail of these rocks is found from Jasper along the western prairies all the way to Northern Montana. This is called the "Foothills Erratic Train."

Just outside the town of Okotoks, Alberta there is a three-story-high boulder, the largest glacial erratic in the world. It weighs about 16,000 tons and is called "Big Rock."

Q q

Rocks tumbled onto a glacier.
They fell from a great height.
The glacier moved them far away.
Q's for erratic Quartzite.

Rr

The Rocky Mountains run along Alberta's western border from the Wilmore Wilderness Park down through Jasper, Banff, Kananaskis, and Waterton.

Two mountainous regions of Alberta are Banff and Jasper. In 1885 Banff National Park, Canada's first national park, was founded with the discovery of the Cave and Basin Hot Springs. In the town of Banff is the famous Banff Springs Hotel, known as the "Castle of the Rockies."

Jasper is the largest national park in the Rocky Mountains of Canada. It is also home to the tallest mountain in Alberta, Mount Columbia, which is 3,954 metres high.

The mountain areas also include emerald green lakes, cascading waterfalls such as those at Johnson and Maligne Canyons, and the Castleguard Caves, the longest in Canada, with passages that go for 20 kilometres.

And **R** is for ratless Alberta. There are no rats in Alberta thanks to the Rocky Mountains, which rats cannot cross, and an extermination program along the Saskatchewan border.

R is for the Rocky Mountains.
Its rugged peaks touch the sky.
Gently covered by a blanket of snow—
silence, but for a hawk's shrill cry.

Out of the gate charges a ranting bull.
Crazed to throw who dares to ride!
Fearless cowboys at S for Stampede
come from across the countryside.

The Calgary Exhibition and Stampede is known as the world's greatest outdoor show. Each year hundreds of cowboys and cowgirls from all over North America come to compete. The first Stampede was held in 1912 with an attendance of 14,000 when Guy Weadick had a vision for Calgary to hold a huge "frontier days" event. Today the attendance is over one million people! The daily rodeo includes exciting events such as bareback horse riding, women's barrel racing, steer wrestling, wild cow milking, and the nearly impossible, unbelievable bull riding! The entire city is alive with festivities and the wonderful western hospitality of Calgarians dressed like cowboys and cowgirls, greeting other folks with a "Howdy!"

T is for Turtle Mountain.
Natives named it "Mountain That Walks."
On the day the mountain collapsed
the town of Frank was under rocks.

Tt

On April 29, 1903, Turtle Mountain crumpled. It was the greatest landslide in North American history. Imagine the sound of rocks cracking and cascading down the mountainside! One hundred million tons of limestone slid into the valley. This avalanche took only 100 seconds to occur! Over a mile of the Canadian Pacific Railway was destroyed and Frank, a town located in Southern Alberta, was almost totally destroyed. Tremors from the mountain occurred often and the miners could shovel up coal as it fell from the ceilings in the mining tunnels. This falling coal was actually a sign of the mountain's eventual collapse. Today the Frank Slide is a huge limestone monument lying at the base of Turtle Mountain.

U u

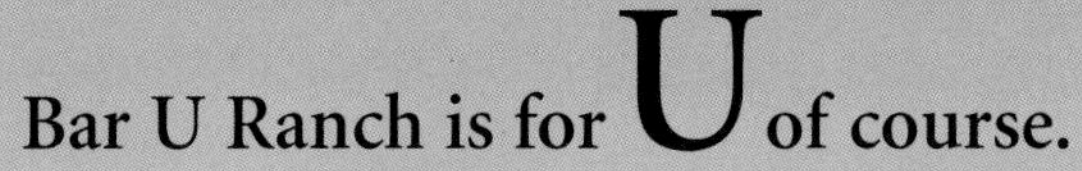

Bar U Ranch is for U of course.
Experience the Canadian west.
A famous working cattle ranch,
one of the largest, one of the best.

The Bar U Ranch is a historic site where you can experience the spirit of the Canadian West. Fred Stinson and the Northwest Cattle Company founded the Bar U Ranch in 1882. Open ranching was practiced until 1902. At that time George Lane took over the ranch and expanded it to an international breeding centre for cattle and Percheron horses. The cowhands lived in bunkhouses and were provided meals, but were paid just once a year. Lane also designed the famous brand Ū.

In 1907 Patrick Burns took control of the ranch. It then became one of Canada's largest working cattle ranches.

In 1991 Parks Canada acquired this ranch that is a 150-hectare facility with 35 historic buildings.

Today Alberta is Canada's largest cattle producing region where 60 percent of the country's beef is produced.

The world's largest Easter egg in Vegreville, Alberta, was built in 1975 to celebrate the 100th anniversary of the formation of the Royal Canadian Mounted Police in Alberta. Pysanka is the name for a Ukrainian Easter egg. The end of the egg has a radiating gold star, symbolizing life and good fortune. This silver, gold, and bronze egg took over 12,000 hours to design and build. The egg has 2,206 triangular pieces. It is actually like a giant jigsaw puzzle!

In 1891 a large colony of Ukrainians settled in Vegreville. This was at a time when the Canadian government was encouraging immigration and settlement to the prairies. Today Vegreville has a population of over 5,000 and is mainly a farming town. It is the largest Ukrainian settlement in Canada.

V v

V is for Vegreville's Pysanka,
the largest Easter egg in the land.
And just to get around it
takes ten people holding hands!

W
w

Alberta's provincial flower is the wild rose and Alberta is known as Wild Rose Country. This small shrub grows 30 to 90 centimetres high and is found on the prairies, roadsides, edges of woods, and along riverbanks. The wild rose blooms in different shades of pink. It is used for making candies, sauces, teas, wine, and even for perfume and medicine.

And **W** is for the golden fields of wheat swaying in the wind and glistening in the sunshine. Alberta has over 59,000 farms including crop, dairy, and cattle farming. Wheat is the primary crop grown in Alberta. Barley, oats, hay, and canola are the next most important crops. Alberta's farms make agriculture the second most important industry in the province next to oil and gas.

W is also for Wood Buffalo National Park, Canada's largest national park. Lying partly in Alberta and partly in the Northwest Territories, this park was established in 1922 to protect the bison herds in Northern Canada.

Our pretty provincial flower
is W for Wild Rose.
It grows across the prairies
and along where rivers flow.

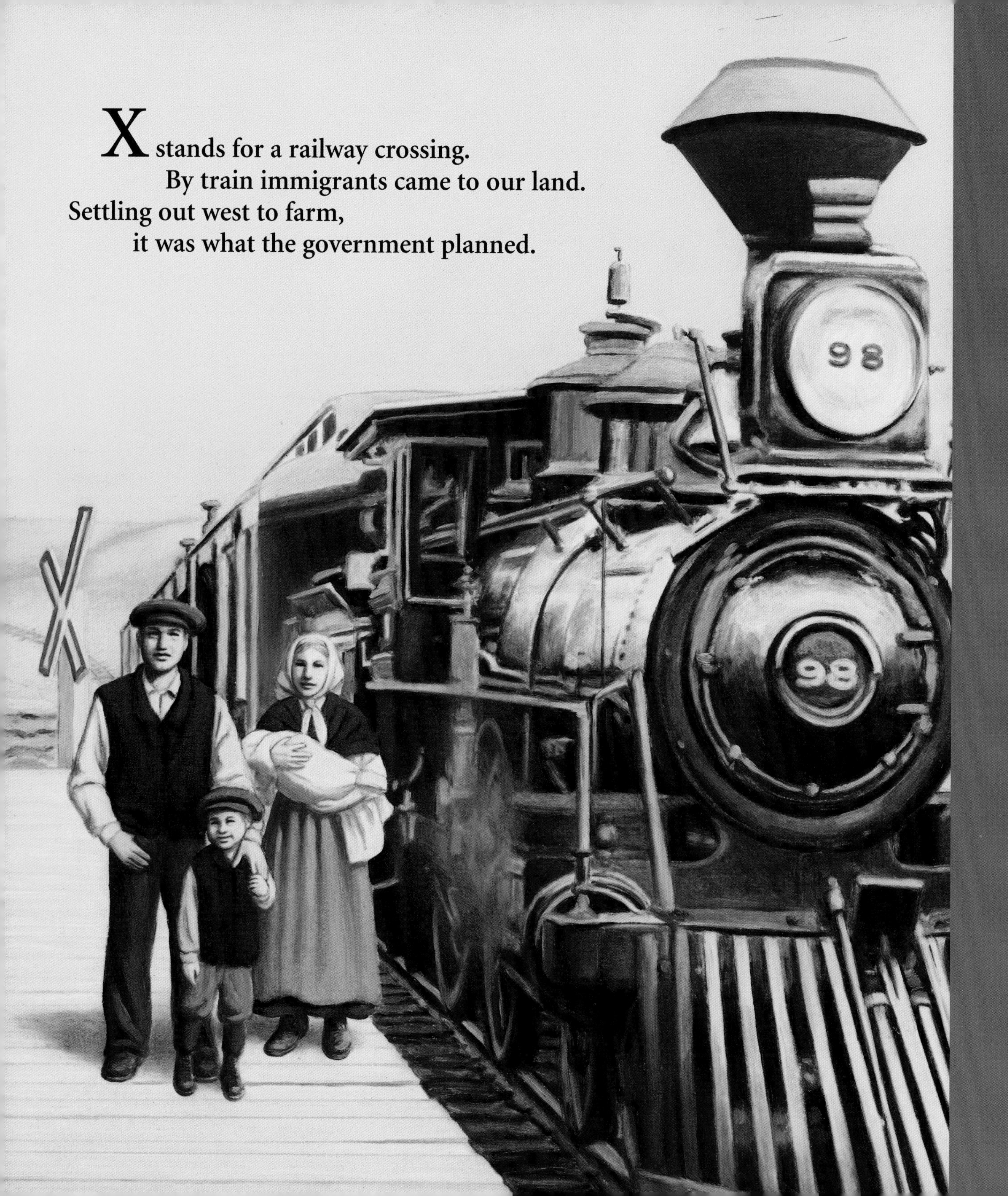

X stands for a railway crossing.
By train immigrants came to our land.
Settling out west to farm,
it was what the government planned.

The first railway to come through Alberta was in 1883. This was the transcontinental Canadian Pacific Railway (CPR). When the Canadian government encouraged immigration and agricultural development, a great many Europeans from many countries came to Alberta. Most settlers in the 1890s farmed wheat. Cattle ranching also began in southwestern Alberta. Not only did the railway provide transportation for settlers to move west, it was the means for moving the grain, cattle, and beef to markets. The railway also had a major effect on the coal industry at Coalbanks (today know as Lethbridge). The arrival of the railway inspired a group to open a coal mine in this area where a narrow railway track was extended from the coal mine to the CPR's main line. This way the coal could be transported.

Because of the railway, millions of acres of farmland, ranchland and new cities and towns were developed in Alberta.

They sing, dance and do acrobatics.
Across the stage they go.
Y is for the "Young Canadians"
performing at the grandstand show.

The talented Young Canadian are from the Calgary area and vary in ages starting as young as seven years old up to 20. Through an audition process the children are taught throughout the year by the Young Canadian School of Performing Arts. These young people are taught voice and singing lessons, dancing and gymnastics, ballet and even acrobatics as well as musical theatre. It is hard work, with 20 hours a week of practice leading up to the big grandstand show for 16,000 people. The Young Canadians perform at Christmas and spring concerts and have travelled to other provincial, state, and world fairs. They have even put on performances for Her Majesty Queen Elizabeth II and the royal family.

The performers also put on a spectacular outdoor variety show during the Calgary Stampede.

Yy

The Calgary Zoo is home to "Destination Africa." Here you can find round thatched grass huts, African music, and rain forests alive with many creatures. Lowland gorillas, colobus monkeys, and ring-tailed lemurs hang from trees and wrestle. Imagine a tank for the hippopotamus that holds water equal to 4,000 bathtubs! Kamala is an Asian elephant at the Calgary zoo that paints pictures. In the wild, elephants use their trunks to pick up sticks or rocks and then draw in the sand and soil. The Calgary Zoo is also famous for its unique Prehistoric Park with man-made land formations, lakes, and life-size dinosaurs. Don't get too close to Rex!

What would you do with zoomanu? Every Mother's Day the Valley Zoo in Edmonton sells compost made from manure of elephants, camels, zebras, and other zoo animals.

Zz

Z is for a safari at the Zoo.
Trek through a steamy rain forest
to see swinging monkeys and lowland gorillas
dwarf crocodiles, lizards, and tortoise.

Prairies to Peaks: Alberta Facts

1. What is the name of the largest body of ice in the Rocky Mountains?
2. In the early 1900s, what famous woman doctor travelled by horseback in Northern Alberta to care for the sick?
3. What are the warm winds called that can melt away all the snow in just hours?
4. What is our provincial mammal? Do you know what the male is called?
5. What is our provincial tree? Do you know what our Natives used this tree for?
6. Who was Anthony Henday?
7. One of Alberta's famous steer wrestling cowboys was named:
8. Do you know what scientists that study prehistoric life-forms are called?
9. "Cat owl" is a nickname for what bird?
10. What is Alberta's provincial stone?
11. What animal did the First Nations in Alberta mainly survive from? What did this animal provide for the people?
12. What is a meat-eating dinosaur called? Can you name one?
13. How did the "Big Rock" (erratic quartzite) end up just outside of Okotoks?
14. How did European immigrants travel to Alberta in 1883?
15. What is Alberta's Provincial Fish?
16. One of the world's largest oil reserves is in Northern Alberta. Can you name it?
17. What mineral was mixed with water and animal grease to make paint? What are the paintings made on the rocks called?
18. What was the greatest landslide in North American history?
19. What is a Ukrainian Easter egg called?
20. Erosion carves soft sandstone into unusual pillar shapes that are called what?
21. How many of the women known as the "Famous Five" are you able to name?
22. What is Alberta's capital?
23. Where is Alberta's highest mountain? Do you know its name?
24. Can you name two rodeo events at the Calgary Stampede?

Answers

1. Columbia Icefield
2. Mary Percy Jackson
3. Chinook winds
4. Bighorn Sheep; ram
5. Lodgepole pine; teepee poles
6. Trader and explorer guided by the Cree Natives
7. John Ware
8. Paleontologists
9. Great horned owl
10. Petrified wood
11. Buffalo; food, shelter, tools, decorations, toys, bedding, utensils
12. Carnivore; *Tyrannosaurus Rex*
13. Moved there by a glacier
14. By train
15. Bull trout
16. Athabasca Tar Sands
17. Iron ore; pictographs
18. Frank Slide
19. Pysanka
20. Hoodoos
21. Emily Murphy, Henrietta Muir Edwards, Nellie McClung, Louise McKinney, Irene Parlby
22. Edmonton
23. Jasper; Mt. Columbia
24. Bull riding, steer wrestling, women's barrel racing, bareback horse riding, wild cow milking

Dawn Welykochy

Dawn Alice Welykochy grew up in Calgary and now lives with her family on a ranch in southern Alberta. In addition to caring for her children, Dawn enjoys their many animals, some of which are emus, llamas, miniature donkeys, and everyone's favourite—a zoni which is a zebra/pony cross.

Dawn attended the University of Calgary where she graduated with a Bachelor of Arts degree in English. She has also recently undergone training to teach Montessori preschool. She looks forward to travelling through Alberta to share *C is for Chinook: An Alberta Alphabet* with schoolchildren.

Lorna Bennett

Lorna Bennett has worked as a designer, writer, illustrator, and animator. Her illustrations in *Sandwiches for Duke* won her a nomination for the Amelia Frances Howard-Gibbon Illustrator's Award. Lorna currently devotes most of her time to artwork for children's picture and educational books, greeting cards, novel covers, technical illustration, multimedia, and animation. Touring with the Young Alberta Book Society's Chrysalis Festival and teaching art in elementary schools has kept Lorna busy for the past several years. She attended Grant MacEwan Community College and the University of Alberta in the Arts/Fine Arts programs.

Lorna is a born and bred Albertan who especially loves mountain biking all year, hiking, literature, music, painting, cooking, travel, and Edmonton's annual Heritage Days Festival.